Piggy and Pug

First edition, second printing, published 2018

Printed in China

ISBN: 978-0-9741160-9-9

Written by Anne Wheaton

Edited by Charlotte Moore

Illustrated by Vipin Alex Jacob

Designed by Will Hindmarch

To my husband, Wil, whose love and support helped motivate me to write the story I'd always wanted to read. And to my friend Ariana Osborne, whose guidance and encouragement helped me turn this story into an actual book.

Pug lived with a young couple in a little blue house on a corner in a tiny town. During the day, while the couple was away at work, Pug would stretch out on the grass to chew on his favorite squeaky toy, followed by an afternoon nap on the front porch.

When his family returned, Pug would leap off the porch and greet them at the front gate. Together, they would go inside for dinner, and afterwards, Pug would get belly rubs and snuggling on the sofa.

Just outside the tiny town, Piggy lived with her family of three in a big red farmhouse surrounded by a huge pasture. In the family was a boy who loved her, fed her, and played with her, but while the boy was away at school, Piggy didn't have anyone to play with.

She spent her days snoozing on the porch, dreaming of finding a friend to share adventures with, until eventually, the boy would return from school and the two of them could play again.

One day, Pug's family put all of their belongings in boxes and suitcases, loaded them into a truck, and drove away. Pug was a good dog, so he sat on the front porch and waited for them to return, as usual.

He waited and waited.
Then he waited some more.
But the truck didn't come back. Soon, Pug was scared and lonely and hungry. But Pug was also brave. So he decided to go in search of a new family.

Pug went up to the gate, pushed his nose on the latch to open it, then walked down the sidewalk and out onto the empty street.

Turning a corner, he passed a produce stand busy with shoppers, and a hardware store where an exiting customer narrowly missed him. Dodging a car as he ran into the street, Pug began down a long dirt road out of the tiny town. It was the longest road he had ever been on.

He felt like he had been walking forever when he spotted a patch of wildflowers, and butterflies frolicking above them. It looked like fun, so Pug ran to join them, shouting, "Will you be my family?"

But as he approached, all of the butterflies scattered. Pug was heartbroken, but decided to keep going. "Oh, well," he said to himself. "Without wings, I suppose I wouldn't be able to keep up with them anyway."

That same day, as Piggy sat on the front porch of the farmhouse, watching the cows in the pasture, she got an idea. She jumped off the porch and skipped over to the cows, shouting, "Will you be my friend?"

The cows didn't look up at Piggy. They just ate the grass at their feet.

But Piggy wasn't about to give up. She kept walking until she spotted a bunch of chickens eating bugs on the ground. She raced over to them, shouting, "Will you be my friend?"

But as she approached, the chickens all ran off in different directions, clucking and scolding her. Frustrated, Piggy stomped her hoof. Wouldn't someone be her friend?

Meanwhile, Pug had continued down the long dirt road until he came upon a pond full of turtles swimming together. They looked like they were having a great time, so Pug ran down to the water to join them, shouting, "Will you be my family?"

But as he approached, the turtles ducked underwater, disappearing from Pug's view. "Oh, well," he said to himself. "I'm not a very good swimmer, so I wouldn't be able to keep up with them anyway."

Pug sighed and continued around the pond. On the other side, he came upon a field so big, he was unable to see where it ended.

Tall grass gently swayed and nearby trees whistled as the breeze blew through the landscape. The sounds made Pug a little nervous, so he walked faster than before.

At the farm, Piggy lay back down on the porch, resting her chin on her foot as she let out a big sigh. It would still be hours before the boy came home from school so they could play together.

She passed the time watching busy ants go in and out of a dirt mound just below the porch. Soon, her eyelids began to droop.

As Pug made his way across the field, he was spotted by a hungry fox lurking in the tall grass. The fox crouched down, sneaking slowly and quietly so Pug wouldn't hear him.

The fox sneaked.
And sneaked.
And sneaked.

Then, when he thought he was close enough, the fox sprinted right for Pug, crashing noisily through the tall grass. Startled, Pug looked over his shoulder and saw the hungry fox coming right for him!

Pug darted off in another direction, running as fast as he could. Soon, he saw a fence up ahead with a small hole in it—it looked like it was big enough for him but too small for the fox.

Pug leaped for the fence, wriggled through the hole, and ran without looking back.

On the porch of the farmhouse, Piggy was sleeping in the sun when a commotion woke her up. She sat up just in time to see Pug running across the pasture. Still groggy from her nap, she watched in stunned silence as Pug headed her way.

When he was sure that the fox hadn't followed him, Pug slowed down to catch his breath.

He realized he had stopped right in front of a farmhouse. It had a porch just like his house had, and on the porch was a pig.

Piggy stood up as she and Pug stared into each other's eyes. She couldn't believe what she was looking at. With a huge smile on her face, Piggy sprang off the porch, landed at Pug's feet, and shouted, "Will you be my friend?"

Startled at first, Pug looked at Piggy; then, bursting with joy, shouted back, "Yes! I will!"

Piggy spent the rest of the day showing Pug all around the farm. They played in mud puddles together, bounced around with frogs, and ran through the sprinklers that watered the pasture.

Soon, they were so tired, Piggy and Pug went back to the farmhouse porch to nap together in the afternoon sun.

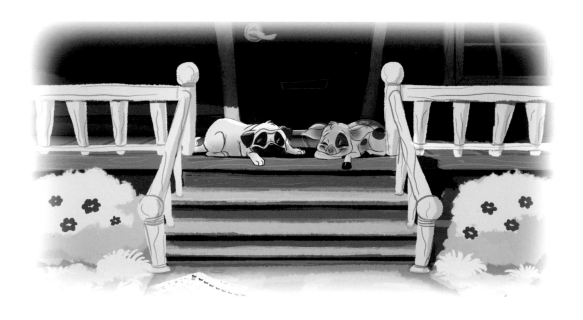

After school, the boy walked home down the long dirt road to the farm. He approached the gate to the pasture and opened it, making his way to the front porch—where he spotted Piggy and Pug napping in the sun.

The boy dropped his school bag. "Dad, Mom!" he cried. "Come quick!" The boy's parents rushed outside, where they saw him crouched down, petting Pug. He looked up at their startled faces. "Can we keep him?"

The boy's father shook his head. "He can't stay, son. That little dog is named Pug. He lives with the Felix family, and they love him, so we should take him back."

This made Piggy, Pug, and the boy very sad, but the boy knew it was the right thing to do, so they all got in the truck and headed back into town.

The four of them drove by the field with the fox and the pond with the turtles, down the long dirt road, and through the little town, until at last they came to Pug's house. There were no cars in the driveway, and no lights on in the windows.

As they walked up to the porch, they saw a sign on the door that said "FORECLOSED." "What does 'foreclosed' mean?" the boy asked. "Well," said the boy's dad, "it means they couldn't afford to stay in the house anymore. I bet they left Pug behind because they couldn't afford to keep him, either."

This confused the boy. "Why didn't they find a new home for Pug instead of abandoning him? I thought they loved him."

The boy's dad sighed. "Some people just don't think of finding a new home for their pets, or taking them to a shelter where they'll get proper care and an opportunity for a new family to adopt them."

This explanation saddened the boy even more. "I hope people won't do that anymore," he said.

He paused. Then he asked, "Can we be Pug's new family?"

His dad thought for a moment. "I know you take very good care of Piggy, so if you're ready to take care of Pug as well, then yes, we can be Pug's new family."

The boy squealed with joy and cried, "Yes! I can do it!" Piggy, Pug, and the boy jumped up and down with excitement. Then they hopped back in the truck and headed home.

That evening, Piggy, Pug, and the boy went for a walk together down to the river, where the boy went fishing while Piggy and Pug played with the bucket of worms he was using for bait.

As darkness filled the air, the three friends made their way back to the farmhouse, while glowing fireflies swooped around their heads like tiny flashlights lighting the way home.

Inside, the boy took Piggy and Pug up to his room, where he made them each a cozy bed on the floor beside his own.

Exhausted from the excitement of the day, they tucked themselves in and fell fast asleep. The night would bring sweet dreams of new adventures yet to come—for the boy, for Piggy, and for Pug, who now had the best new family and friends he could have ever hoped for.

The end.

About Anne Wheaton

When I was 5, an orange tabby cat followed me home from a friend's house. After two days of searching for his owners, we discovered that they had moved away and left this cat behind. He had gone out in search of a new family, and we became that for him. This began my lifelong commitment of adopting rescue animals into our family, and is why I have supported the Pasadena Humane Society & SPCA for the past 8 years, 4 of them as a board member. I live in Los Angeles with my husband, Wil, and our three rescue pets. I wrote this book because it's something little-kid-me would have wanted to read.

You can find me on Twitter and Instagram at @AnneWheaton, and on my blog: AnneWheaton.com

About Vipin Alex Jacob

I couldn't help myself. As a child, I drew on every scrap of paper I could find. My house walls were large canvases for characters conjured from my imagination. My earliest influences were Disney and Warner Brother Cartoons, especially *The Jungle Book* and *The Lion King*. Growing up, I coupled two of my greatest passions—drawing and storytelling—in animation. Now I work as an art director for an animation studio in Toronto, Ontario, where I have the greatest pleasure bringing characters and worlds to life.

You can find me online at: artstation.com/vipinjacob